Settling Down

IRA SADOFF

Settling Down

1975

HOUGHTON MIFFLIN COMPANY BOSTON

FIRST PRINTING W

Copyright © 1975 by Ira Sadoff

Library of Congress Cataloging in Publication Data

Sadoff, Ira.   Settling down.

    I. Title.
PS3569.A26S4   811'.5'4   74-20848
ISBN 0-395-20288-4   ISBN 0-395-20361-9 pbk.

Printed in the United States of America

To Dianne, Jim and Paul

Acknowledgment is made to the following publications for poems or versions of poems which have appeared in them:

The American Poetry Review: "Alienation of Affection," "My Last Two Wives"; *Antaeus:* "Melancholy"; *The Antioch Review:* "For Ecology," "In the Butcher Shop," "Kafkaesque," "The Last Train of Thought," "Seance," "A Search for the Voice," "Settling Down," "The Sky Is Falling," "There Are Twenty-six Versions," "The Thirties"; *Carolina Quarterly:* "Take One"; *Denver Quarterly:* "The French Film"; *Epoch:* "After Hearing That Man Descends from the Killer Ape"; *The Iowa Review:* "My Last Three Wives"; *Kayak:* "A Concise History of the World"; *The Little Magazine:* "Dada Poem"; *New American Review:* "Disease of the Eye," "Soap Opera"; *New York Quarterly:* "Dream of a Drugstore in a Bookstore"; *North American Review:* "Carpentry"; *Open Places:* "Lovesong," "Role Reversal," "Steam"; *The Paris Review:* "Hopper's 'Nighthawks' (1942)," "Last Meeting," "On Meeting Robert Desnos in My Sleep," "An Open Letter to My Wife," "Seurat," "The Revolution of 1905," "1928"; *Poetry:* "Four Variations on the History of Speech"; *Poetry Northwest:* "Acknowledgments," "Love Poem"; *Shenandoah:* "The Shape of Content," "The Return to Mysticism"; *Skywriting:* "The Great Chain of Being"; *Sumac:* "A Yaqui Way to Knowledge"; *Virginia Quarterly Review:* "On the Fainting of Freud."

CONTENTS

III. *Going Back to Sleep*

One

Waiting for Evening

"And the clouds flew round and the clouds flew round and the clouds flew round with the clouds."
— WALLACE STEVENS, "The Pleasures of Merely Circulating"

"Idleness is the beginning of all psychology."
— NIETZSCHE, *Twilight of the Idols*

Settling Down

A change comes over me.
My wife and I no longer speak.
The newspaper yellows in my hands
like tobacco stains. All day I sit
at my desk watching the tea steep
in its cup, the copper blood
running out of its sack
like fluid from a dying fish.
I no longer hear the noise
of the neighbors, the husbands
begging to be set free, the wives
asking them to go. The lovers
walk by my house in silence
as if they knew no human voice
could please me. What is happening
to my ears has already happened
to the rest of my body. It is a kind
of rest that settles onto the skin
like dust, it is the kind of dust
that comes out of the body after death.

Soap Opera

Someone is always dying.

The father is always an alcoholic.
The mother hates her children.
A young girl is often raped
by her own brother.
A long lost brother loses
his memory.

It is always raining.
Everything happens inside.
A close friend has a nervous breakdown.
Complete strangers break up completely
happy marriages.
A wealthy relative has a heart attack.

One man is always strong enough to stand up
against all this. He is taken off the air.

Melancholy

A snowstorm in the middle of May!
You sit by the window, chin
on palm, listening to the sparrows
calling from behind the snowdrifts,
watching the black ash of the
butterfly wilting on the branches.

Nothing can penetrate this sadness —
a basket of flowers would be good
for the dead. A thaw would turn the earth
to mud. When your wife calls you down
to dinner, your meal is like the fresh
meat of the locust, the milk
is blue as your mother's breast.

The gauze of the curtains is an eyelid
between you and the world,
some vague impression: a flotilla
of grasses sinking in the snow,
a moon without shadow, a bee
collapsing at the heart of the flower.

Carpentry

It feels so good
hammering
the eyes of nails

the center of the house
I am holding up
a kind of power

like a bone in the fist,
someone who owns the world
he lives in — it is not

easy, it is not
what I have been
with others, small

as the circle
in my eyes, lids
I have never opened.

This is a real house
I live in, it keeps
my family close as

my breath, and like it
they move in and out
of me, all when I hold

this hammer, this hammer
in my hand is like an eye:
it breaks everything it sees.

Role Reversal

We speak through a drainpipe.
You lie in a hammock
while I take dictation.
We live in a studio.
You are the artist
and I am the model.
I make obscene poses
while you paint black shadows
under your eyelids.
Or we lie on the canvas.
You wrestle me to the ground
and I go down for the count.
The dishes pile up like old letters.
You write *I love you*
in the tomato sauce.
My day is made.
I can stand at the sink
and dream of walking on the moon
with my spatula, while
you fly out the window
with my younger sister.

An Open Letter to My Wife

I must confess to everything.
My passion for leeches.
The rose
tattooed to your thighs.
Certain fragrances I cannot mention.
My hatred of symmetries:
the blackbird balanced
on the ear of the cow,
the pig aslant
against the rows of corn.

A certain need to destroy
parts of me that will not grow.
An unnatural fear of strangers.
My greatest ambition has been to pass
through water like the sun through glass.
I would hear music everywhere.

Whatever happened is always hard
to say: I fell out of favor
with my loved ones. I was exposed
to certain unpleasant tasks.
I refused to ask for help.
Then I lost my sense of direction.
Birds flew through me.
Open windows made me leap
from my skin, and the rain
made me weep for days on end.
Now I am like a stone

at the bottom of a canyon.
A voice at the end of a tunnel.

Those who love me still
will never see me otherwise.

My Last Two Wives

My last two wives loved everything
about potatoes their ugly color their hopeless
shape they even loved the joke about potatoes
"What has a thousand eyes but cannot see?"
they loved to mash them
fry them boil them until they cried out for help
they loved to cut them open
just to see the cold cup of starch
lying still in its skin like a snowdrift

they could not live without potatoes
it was amazing like a bad habit
they could not stop
from grabbing potatoes off the counters
hiding them in their pocketbooks
and dreaming of endless tables of potatoes
weeping out of all their eyes
caressing them into sleeplessness
making them eat their own dirt

it is a wonder I could not love them

My Last Three Wives

I left my last three wives
incognito I grew a mustache
I gave them all false names
you were the provocateur
you the conspirator
and you were the indigent

now I throw wild parties
dancing around the wedding rings
blowing smoke through all the holes
nothing makes me happy anymore

all day I walk down the corridors
knocking on the widows' doors
asking them "Who can compare with the dead?"

I hate all these mirrors and the smoke
in the lobby all this waiting
for love makes me nervous
someone is unwriting the messages meant for me
tying the telephone up in knots

so now I have to climb the treetops
looking in all the windows
on one floor I am making conversation
on another I seem to be making love
what a way to pass the time

watching a man take off his pants
putting out a cigarette
hoping someone will discover me

The French Film

never leaves the bedroom.
Even at breakfast
the lovers contain their hunger.
The man wants only a cigarette.
"So early in the morning," the woman moans.
He offers her a puff, but only one.

Someday, she knows, he will leave her
for someone else. But for now
he cannot take his eyes off her body.
When he reaches out for her
breasts, the camera lifts its head.
The sheets rustle like conversation.
In the background Charles Aznavour
weeps freely on the phonograph.
The telephone rings. The bathtub overflows.
Lying still on the table, the coffee
is black as a nightshade and just as cold.
The last croissant unfurls,
flaking, as always, at the corners.

Acknowledgments

My mother was first:
when I popped out and forgot
to say thank you I never
heard the end of it. Then
my father whacked the thank
you right out of me. To my
first friends I am forever
thankful for seeing me
through the worst of times,
they always told me when
my shoes were all wrong,
and when I went too far.
I can never thank my
first girl friend enough:
she taught me not to let myself
go in her presence, but I let
myself go anyway, and she,
thank you, let me go faster
than I could say I'm sorry.
I don't want to forget the
government to whom I am
endlessly thankful. I could not
thank my wife in her presence.
And since we have no children
to thank, there is just enough
time to thank the world for
letting us visit, and taking us
out of it just when we learn
we can almost live without it.

Lovesong

I love the luxury of boredom,
the long white robe lying
on the davenport, the lace
curtains blocking out the sun,
a room full of smoke and empty
ashtrays. This year has been
a Sunday spent without regret,
a long morning stretched
out in bed, a close look
at the fingernails, the shades
never pulled completely down. The news
in the papers is sad: a king
has been shot by his own
army, so many trains are off
the track, the flowers have come up
and died. The last time I tried
to get out of bed I fell
into a coma, I saw this weather
forever, a cloud in the shape
of a mouth, a long horizon, a thirsty
sky that could never be filled.

The Mathematician's Disclaimer

What I would give for a clear field
of vision, to rid myself of the crippling
disorder of my desk, my only child
standing before my wife, the wild
grass growing slowly over my shoetops.
I have given my life to numbers, and these
numbers, in return, have given me a life
I cannot control. But that is all
beside the point. Nothing is really solved:
as the photograph resolves in its pan,
the plan to map the path of the sun
cannot be won. What a relief to know
that if my days are numbered I have numbered
them myself, the pleasure in the music
of my life is not left in the clock, nor
the tock of the metronome, but in the moment
between moments, the measure left unmeasured.

Feeling and Form

Nothing can be done about
the redundancy of shape: your ass
in a sling, the duplicity of lips,
the policeman walking with his walking
stick. Even our speech redoubles itself:
talking in circles is not so much talking
to ourselves, but taking the subject
and subjecting it to our sense
of separation. We bury the incongruity
of our wishes, the split infinitive
stays under the tongue: the secret desire
to flatten the world, to change the shape
of one's wishes, to make oneself whole
without closing the circle forever.

The Shape of Content

All winter we said we were waiting
for winter to end. Now we are waiting
for someone to tell us when to begin.

We stretch our arms, our legs, our days
into long nights without sleep. "What
can we do?" we are always asking ourselves,

and like everybody we know, nobody
knows the answer. A Buddhist monk
once told me I should empty myself

like a pail of water, a filled toilet.
I asked him what did he know about
what the month of December does to a man,

and when I took everything out of my body,
even all the words I never said, I was left
looking at you, a woman with her tongue

in my mouth, her fingers counting the days
left to live this year, her eyes circling
like a flock of geese with nowhere to land.

Tonight

I resist all temptation.
My wife
lying in bed beside me,
the refrigerator with its hum
of hunger, the open closets
with their coats waiting to be filled.

I want to remain
pure as sleep. In my dream
I wear the white coat
of the doctor — when I turn
down the sheets I see clouds
of flesh rising up
to the ceiling, the bones
walking out on the body
like an angry mistress.
Only the illness remains
like the yolk of an egg
shining at the heart of everything.

Love Poem

1.

Who could take another spring
like this, the starlings
nesting in the pines like black
fruit, the dark blood
of the grass beginning to flow
again, the white stars
of the snow digging their graves
in the sea of mud.

2.

The flowerbeds are swollen with water.
The drainpipes overflow with leaves
and twigs, the bodies of small insects
are sliding down the shingles.
The slow rain is everywhere.

3.

Yesterday my wife took off
her clothes for the first time
in a week. The light
from her body glowed like the red
lamp of the darkroom. When I touched her
breasts I could see my bones
shining through the cups of the palms.
Her eyes were like pockets
of midnight, her stare went through me
like a tongue of black secrets. What sun
could fly through the body
like this, what rain, which dark birds?

Take One

I am the sheriff lifting
up your dress. You are queen
of the cafes. There isn't a man
in the house who hasn't bought you
a drink. When I wear my white
hat, I fill my mouth with bourbon
and valor. I pretend to be talking
to the bartender. "You ought to be
ashamed of this life," I tell
them all. "What do you want
from me?" you ask. "Nothing
you can give me," I answer.

The silence on the set is for
whichever one of us has forgotten
his lines. The lights go out
forever, someone takes the tables
and chairs, the cameras break
their lenses. Now we are alone,
we are really alone without a word
to say to each other. What
do you want from me you say
again, and again I say nothing
you can give me. So you give me
the nothing you gave everyone
else. We decide to forget what
could have been said, there's nothing
important about this life
we're in, we can always take
another take, we can always take

Last Meeting

The day begins with a fog
that will not unroll. The weather
is falling everywhere, everywhere
we sit the grass bleeds to the touch.

What we have not yet said will not
get said. When you unzip your dress
a thousand insects run for cover,
the goldenrod breaks into a slow swoon.

Your touch is like the touch
of the wasp undulating in its nest,
your tongue the quick lash
of a mirror breaking on the wrist.

Everything else can wait, but will not.

Two

Forgetting This World

"Though we live in the world we are not carrying on
a worldly war."

— PAUL, *II Corinthians* 10:3

"He who holds me by a thread is not strong; the thread
is strong."

— PORCHIA, *Voices*

A Concise History of the World

Columbus discovered America.
If you lived here before
him, you'd be sadly mistaken.

The same thing with Africa.
Before Diaz rounded the Cape, natives
provided background for the stars.

Edison, of course, harnessed light
into a tiny bulb. Everywhere else
around him had to be called dark.

Civilization is the clean sheet
on an empty bed. Before
marriage, no one made love.

All the Puritans really wanted
was freedom, the freedom to erase
the body before it spread to other places.

People in Red China want to take over
the world. We do not recognize them.
Yellow is really white not feeling

well. It is a little known fact
that people are not really poor:
they are just not hungry

enough to work. Let's face it:
anyone who is not me is mistaken
or my enemy. This is why we choose

up sides. On our side we have
truth. Your side is only human.
We will have to stamp you out.

1928

We are sitting by the pool on a sunny day. You are wearing your white suit, holding a drink in one hand and shading your eyes from the sun with the other. Last night's party has just ended. There are splinters of broken glass gleaming in the sunlight, chaise lounges aslant, a spray of napkins spread over the lawn. Last night we went swimming in the pool with all our clothes on, it was the night you slept with the manufacturer's wife. We never met the host. Nothing could stop the band from playing our song over and over again. All night you talked about your work, how the market would go up and up, how there was nothing to lose no matter how great the risk. The women loved you for that. A strong wind blew in from the bay, but it did not so much as ruffle your hair. The wheels of the Chrysler spun freely in a ditch.

The ugliest men fell all over me. They could not keep their hands off my breasts. I could not count how many of their wives did not understand them, how many of their mistresses had not been faithful to them. I had nightmares of stillborn children and our house on the Cape burning into a small pile of ash. Still, it was comforting to wake up and find you were not beside me. And it was difficult to find you in such a big house: when I walked out of our room I saw a hundred men pacing on the balustrade in long white robes. The women had let their hair down but no one seemed to notice. The rustle of their nightgowns was like the gnawing of termites.

Now my red dress seems too harsh against the clear blue of the pool. We do not speak, but I know you are thinking it is a shame we cannot live this way — you do not have the means and I do not have the desire. You are a little bit sad because the party is over and we have nowhere to go. The women you love are lesbians, and everything you say rubs them the wrong way. The day you try to leave me I will take you for everything you have, I will let you know I never loved you, nothing you can ever do would hurt me.

Love Poem for Imperialists

Everything was barren before I met you.
I could hardly use a napkin, wash my face.
Who knew the difference between a fork
and a plate? So you taught me how to speak
and I didn't have to move my lips.
You brought me gifts I did not refuse.
When we slept together you offered me
advice, technical assistance. You said,
"Never get on top." You took away my hands
because you said you knew how to use them.
You told me I've never been better off.
I was so helpless I couldn't live without you,
but now I'm just mad enough to fight:
I want everything you ever gave me
back, and more. You may be too tired
to love me, but you're not too fat to run.

On Hearing That Man Descends
from the Killer Ape

I shave the hair off my face.

I walk the streets
erect, making sounds
like sentences. Nobody knows

I came from a jungle
of hair and was covered
by my mother's blood.

Nobody knows
I eat the flesh
of women at night.

I dream of men underwater
trying to say, "I am
a man," and drowning

in their own words.
This is the secret I try
keeping from myself. Only

at night, when I can hear
the roots growing, do I smother
myself under the blankets like an ape

dropped into the sea, tied to a rock.
And when I speak, the words come out
like bubbles of air rising to the surface.

The Sky Is Falling

The old whirlpool is stirring again.
The flowers are folding up
their petals, birds are diving
into the windows, the preachers
are pleading for the dust
to return. They predict that sin
will spill out of the bedrooms
into our political life.
The Mayor is undressing the members
of his council, the tractors
are rolling the city into a ball
of dirt. Someone has made a terrible
mistake. In the clouds the distance
is moving like a picture out of focus.

Somewhere out there someone is watching
over this entire affair — he knows
if someone has pulled the plug
out of this world, we are only
sinking into the next. If someone
has broken the great chain
of being, we can always send it
out for repairs, chalk it up
to the world of experience.

The Thirties

The cars are all black.
The men wear hats
and the women long dresses
simply to cover themselves.

The only sound is the radio,
the muffled sound of the voice
gagged in a handkerchief:
it says, "This is not your life."

Buildings empty like slashed wrists.
The streets are paved with hands,
and money flows through the fingers
like rain in a desert or a great fire.

My father walks these streets.
He does not look for work. He waits
for the anarchist to leap from the hallways
to plant a bomb inside him: he will sit

in a crowded theater and go off
just as the hero is cured of
an incurable disease. The bodies will spray
out as an enormous fountain, a bouquet

of arms and legs. This is a dream
of the thirties: to explode into a circle
of strangers, to open every part of yourself
in the dark without hope.

Hopper's "Nighthawks" (1942)

Imagine a town where no one walks the streets. Where the sidewalks are swept clean as ceilings and the barber pole stands still as a corpse. There is no wind. The windows on the brick buildings are boarded up with doors, and a single light shines in the all-night diner while the rest of the town sits in its shadow.

In an hour it will be daylight. The busboy in the diner counts the empty stools and looks at his reflection in the coffee urns. On the radio the announcer says the allies have won another victory. There have been few casualties. A man with a wide-brimmed hat and the woman sitting next to him are drinking coffee or tea; on the other side of the counter a stranger watches them as though he had nowhere else to focus his eyes. He wonders if perhaps they are waiting for the morning buses to arrive, if they are expecting some member of their family to bring them important news. Or perhaps they will get on the bus themselves, ask the driver where he is going, and whatever his answer they will tell him it could not be far enough.

When the buses arrive at sunrise they are empty as hospital beds — the hum of the motor is distant as a voice coming from deep within the body. The man and woman have walked off to some dark street, while the stranger remains fixed in his chair. When he picks up the morning paper he is not surprised to read there would be no exchange of prisoners, the war would go on forever, the Cardinals would win the pennant, there would be no change in the weather.

For Ecology

I write on both sides of the page.
I do not wash my clothes.
I do not throw shit in the water,
and if I could help it I would not
shit at all. I will not buy products
from people who throw shit in the water.
There are no chemicals in my garden.
I do not eat rice
without thinking of the Vietnamese
whose rice is full of our chemicals.
I give the President the finger.
I do not drive a car
that works very often. I often walk
to work when it is not raining.
I dump coke bottles on the lawn
of General Motors. I curb my dog
on the lawn of General Motors.
I give the President the finger.
I read the papers and weep.
I give the finger to the President.

Dada Poem

Whoever broke the policeman's neck
as a symbolic act will never get away
from the man with the bowler hat
full of microphones he puts behind our ears
while we sleep he listens to everything
we hear before we can hear it we cannot escape
the shadow he leaves under our footprints
our mouths will be filled with invisible dust
spraying whatever we say all over
the walls if it is against the law
the walls will crumble what kind of world would we have
then what if everybody wanted to kill a policeman
for a hobby the criminals would be let loose
to commit crimes all over their bodies
it would not be a sight fit for our children to see
this breakdown of law it would be like finding out Hegel
went without underwear we could not go on
living in the chaotic key of g minor
there is a song about love without any words
we could never get anyone to sing it we would
have to chain the men to the night tables to make sure
they were doing it for love and not just
for fun there must be a way of doing away with all this
freedom sweeping it under the carpet like the unwanted
guest who broke up your marriage again
this is the last time we will let him in
our house surely it is against the rules
we are going to make up if we have to

The Revolution of 1905

You are watching a film of the Revolution of 1905. Snow is falling slowly, but in swirls. There is some confusion on the screen; you watch the peasants moving back and forth, catch glimpses of their clothing: the long, rippling capes, the muslin shoes, the babushkas, those strangely-peaked hats. Every so often you see a face: a skeleton with skin, an open mouth, a row of teeth no longer straight. You have the feeling of hunger, but not hunger itself. Your grandfather is in this crowd, huddled behind a woman he does not know. His wife and children must be somewhere else. You know he is supposed to escape from here, but you do not see how. More and more people fill up the screen, until it is no longer possible to see your grandfather's face, his bulky overcoat, the outline of his body . . .

When the czar arrives the audience is still, as though he had the power to become flesh. This is a silent film, so when the czar speaks a card covers the screen. It says, "I decree the death of one hundred, no, two hundred workers." The workers put their hands in front of their faces; this is the film-maker's image of fear, his idea of a dog with his tail between his legs, of the hiss of a cat. "But we have done nothing," the next card says, and then there is a picture of the czar, silent, smiling broadly, the snow forming a thin ridge along his shoulders. In the next frame the peasants have disappeared, there is only the snow, and in the background, coming from the factory's brick chimneys, a banner of smoke that covers the screen like fog. Then a picture of the palace steps, the white marble, whiter than sunlight, the people falling down those steps, the soldiers pointing their rifles, a soldier playing a trumpet, another a drum, and in the distance a wolf howling, a clearing, a forest of birch trees.

Somehow later there is no snow. There is a march in front of the palace, arms raised in victory, although victory does not seem possible. You do not see your grandfather in the crowd, but then again, you do not see him lying dead in the streets. You know you have missed something, but what? When the film ends the audience walks out of the theater single file, as though they were part of an enormous funeral procession. As always, the sunlight outside is too harsh for your eyes. You walk home to your own children, and you have the feeling of sorrow, but not sorrow itself.

There Are Twenty-six Versions

There are twenty-six versions of this story.

•   •   •   •   •   •

Someone is harassing the chief of police.
The sirens are whining for help.
Even the clubs are turning themselves in-
to trees again. Nothing remains the same.

The rocks are freeing the pterodactyls
from the dead. Stars are breaking out
of the sky and someone is playing music
in the spheres. All our clothes are unraveling.

A picture is taking a man of all this.
In the negative he is still a man
turned inside out. His bones are black.
His mouth is no longer an empty space.

•   •   •   •   •   •

There are eighteen more versions of this story.
Soon no one will be able to hurt you.

Alienation of Affection

Picture the end of the War. It is late summer, 1945, and soldiers are still pouring out of the trains like a waterfall. You are sitting on a suitcase with your summer dress, your legs crossed, your lipstick smeared like a falling comet. You are waving to all the men with your tiny flag, wondering which one of them will notice you first, which one will speak to you and what will he say?

You are so glad the War is over, it will mean the end of all this senseless killing, now there will be men walking the streets of your small town, you will no longer have excuses for spending so much time by yourself, for waking up in the middle of the night with those horrible nightmares. You think you will never forget this day, the headlines in the newspapers, the arrangement of the clouds, even the confetti falling from the tallest buildings: all of this means your life will never quite be the same.

But the sight of all those khaki uniforms moving together like a shifting of the earth, stampeding and tripping over one another, brushing past you, begins to make you dizzy. You try to compose yourself but you cannot, so you grab a soldier's arm to keep your balance: he is blonde, a Germanic-looking corporal, and the flatness of all his features makes you think that he must have once been a farmer. He puts his arm around your waist to steady you and in a few moments he is proposing marriage; he says you are the first woman he has touched in eighteen months. Nothing surprises you, and although everything you have been taught tells you otherwise,

you cannot help but accept. So for the rest of your life you
will be dreaming uncontrollably of going to war, of maiming
the enemy, of lying prostrate in your negligee on some
strange battlefield.

Three

Going Back to Sleep

"That what in sleep thou didst abhor to dream,
Waking thou never wilt consent to do."

— MILTON, *Paradise Lost*

Disease of the Eye

Sometimes I wake up in the middle of the night,
In the middle of my own house, to discover
Some woman has had her clothes in my closet
For years. She has even slept in my bed.

I feel like a child in an old movie,
Asking myself where have I been. A film
Covers the eye, and I can only recount events
Out of sequence, in a haze. This is not clear

Enough. It is as though I were a doctor
Looking into my eyes with a strange
Light, chasing the pupil into an endless tunnel
Which is not endless. The pupil shrinks

Like a schoolchild who does not know
The answer. I demand to know everything
Below the skin. Who is the stranger sleeping
In my hands? What does a wife mean at night?

Something strange is going on
In my bed. I ask my wife, "Who is this man
You married?" She answers, "He has eyes that run
Behind the lid." For this ailment

The doctor recommends the following:
Cover the eyes with a cold compress of hands.
The stranger will disappear. The lights
Will dim, but you will know where you have been.

Steam

It hangs on the windows
like a coat of water.
It leaves your mouth in winter
like old secrets. In your tea
it rises to the face of a genie.
It falls backwards
from the lakes and rivers.
You can see it breaking
out of the skin of horses
after a hard run in the rain.
It rests in the bedroom
on the buttocks of your wife.
It gathers itself in the corner
of your eye, and waits for
the trigger of sadness to drop.
There is even steam in sleep.
It covers the eye like a dream
of drowning, it takes shape
on the forehead like a mirage.
It brings you the promise
of waking late at night
with rain on your fingers
or an incredible thirst
for everything you can touch.

Seurat

It is a Sunday afternoon on the Grand Canal. We are watching the sailboats trying to sail along without wind. Small rowboats are making their incisions on the water, only to have the wounds seal up again soon after they pass. In the background the smoke from the factories and the smoke from the steamboats merges into tiny clouds above us then disappears. Our mothers and fathers walk arm and arm along the shore clutching tightly their umbrellas and canes. We are sitting on a blanket in the foreground, but even if someone were to have taken a photograph of us only our closest relatives would have recognized us: we seem to be burying our heads between our knees.

I remember thinking you were one of the most delicate women I had ever seen. Your bones seemed small and fragile as a rabbit's. Even so, beads of perspiration begin to form on your wrist and forehead — if we were to live long enough I'm sure we would have been amazed at how many clothes we forced ourselves to wear. At this time I had never seen you without your petticoats, and if I ever gave thought to such a possibility I would chastise myself for not offering you enough respect.

The sun is very hot. Why is it no one complains of the heat in France? There are women doing their needlework, men reading, a man in a bowler hat smoking a pipe. The noise of the children is absorbed by the trees. The air is full of idleness, there is the faint aroma of lilies coming from somewhere. We discuss what we want for ourselves, abstractly, it seems only right on a day like this. I have ambitions to be a painter, and you want a small family and a cottage in the country. We make everything sound so simple because we believe everything is still possible. The small tragedies of our parents have not yet made an impression on us. We should be grateful for this, but we are too awkward to think hard about very much. I throw a scaling rock into the water; I have strong arms and before the rock sinks it seems to have nearly reached the other side. When we get up we have a sense of our own importance. We could not know, taking a step back, looking at the total picture, that we would occupy such a small corner of the canvas, and that even then we are no more than tiny clusters of dots, carefully placed together without touching.

Kafkaesque

Someone steals the keys.
There are no witnesses
but K. is being held
responsible. He is told
he must give up his job
at ———————.
He does not know why
but he must assure them
there has been a terrible mistake.

There is a telephone call.
He hears the voice of a strange
woman. She wants to take him
away where he can never be
found. She fills the empty cups
of the telephone with loving
promises of escape. He agrees
to meet her in a dark cafe.

Then there is the dream.
It is an old dream of a cafe
opening into a tunnel that turns
inside the woman's legs. On her
thighs is written the mysterious
shape of her face. When they kiss
her mouth drifts off her face
like a leaf. The branches break
off her body when they touch.
Soon there is nothing left

to be desired. He is left alone
in his room. They come for him.
He agrees to tell them everything
they have ever dreamed of,
of the woman who must have taken
him away, of the open doors
to his heart, and of the keys
that must never be found.

A Yaqui Way of Knowledge

First I turn into a coyote.
Then I suck everything out
of the cactus until my hair
bristles like white lightning.

I run around in circles
following the tails of stars
to some other world where
dogs howl at the people

who have lost their way. Somewhere
out there in the desert there
is a dog waiting for me, he
has my name dripping

from his tongue like a meal
he almost had, and if
we howled at the moon together
we'd find a whole new world

between the spaces of our teeth.

Dream of a Drugstore in a Bookstore

I dream the dream of Lana Turner.
Someone will discover me reading
in a bookstore and say, "Hey,
I read your poems in the smallest
magazine I've ever seen. I'd
like to publish your entire body
of work, every poem in your
repertoire. You'll be famous,
people will ask you to write poems
for their birthdays, the President
will ask your advice on foreign
policy, who should we let go
hungry, who should we bomb
tomorrow? You won't even have to write
the poems yourself, there are hundreds
of guys who have your style, who
would ever know the difference?
How could you turn this down
for your miserable life in Ohio,
who would notice you in the museums,
who'll pay the bills for all those
rolls of typewriter ribbon? Do you
really think paper grows on trees?
Why don't you confess, you want to see
your name in lights, you only write
poems for your immediate family,
no one will miss you when you're
gone, there will be no poems
etched on your gravestone, none

in the halls of history, not even
your mother will remember
your name. When you dream the dream
of Lana Turner, you want to tap-
dance on the stars, you want
to write a poem even God
might like, given the chance."

On the Fainting of Freud

After hearing Jung disclose his belief in the collective uncon-
scious, Freud angrily declared that this was Jung's revolt
against the father figure, and proceeded to faint.

— New York Times Magazine

We all have dreams. And some of these dreams
happen again and again like journeys back
to the homeland. On some of these journeys
we meet old friends, our fathers, the earth
we used to bury ourselves in.
So we should not wonder if we might
share these dreams with others, even
the dead. For the dead dream of us
in their way: they see us on the other side
of the earth. And if there is some ridge
on the inner eye where we meet in our sleep,
we should pass without blinking, we should bow
and wish them well, for we travel the same road.

The Acceptance of the Body

The kapellmeister sleeps with the sausage.

A man buried too deeply in thought will lose his hair.

Nuns are unable to sleep in pairs.

The nightmare runs away with the nightingale.

The white chain of sheets flows freely off the balcony.

The slow blade of the eyelid reveals the moat of darkness.

Those who remove their clothes in sleep will not be cold.

The nightmare runs away with the nightgown.

Nuns are unable to sleep alone.

A man may commit suicide with a pillow.

No man can kill himself with his own hands.

The mattress is a permanent fixture of darkness.

A nun may fall asleep in a supermarket.

The slow blade of the eyelid will sever the seed of light.

The nightmare runs away with itself leaving its blankets behind.

Three Dreams of an Ambitious Man

1.

At first you feel safe in the middle of a crowd. Then the magician calls you up to the stage. He tells you that he has chosen you to be his vase, that no matter how many buckets of water he pours down your throat, you will never have enough to drink. In the end you will discover the true meaning of thirst.

2.

You are driving on a superhighway and you press your foot all the way down on the accelerator. The speedometer says that you are breaking the speed limit, but the other cars all pass you by. The other drivers look familiar to you but you cannot place their faces. When you open the window and shout, "Do you remember me?" a tremendous wind rushes over your body, but no one answers you. You blow the horn but even you cannot hear it. In the middle of the highway the car seems to come to a halt; you try to open the doors but cannot.

3.

You and your wife are entertaining close friends. The atmosphere is gay and everyone has a lot to drink. You begin to speak uncontrollably, there is no way you can stop yourself. You admit things to your friends that you would never admit to yourself, that you have never found a job that suited you, you have never been able to tell people how you really feel about them. Your whole life has been a lie. At that moment it seems to you that you have revealed the most intimate details of your life; you feel like an extremely religious man confessing to a priest. You begin to see a dark curtain between yourself and the others in the room. When you are finally able to stop yourself you hear them talking about a subject totally unrelated to you, as if you had not yet entered the room. You shout, you jump up and down, but they do not recognize you. Through the curtain you can see your friend making love to your wife in the presence of his own wife. You want to stop them but you cannot rise out of your chair. You pull open the curtain, but behind that curtain is another curtain, and behind that another and still another. It never occurs to you that it is useless to go on.

A Search for the Voice

It is not in my throat.
You cannot hear it
when I move my lips.
It appears before me
like smoke then bursts
into flame like a fire
burning backwards.

It is the child
that speaks only
to strangers, it is dark
as an empty tunnel.

I will not allow it
to appear in my poems.
It never obeys me.
Sometimes I can keep it
under the paper: these poems
I send to you like a record
without grooves, a documentary
of my silence.

Four Variations on the History of Speech

I have seen the sabotage of the body,
whole armies of language moving upwards
from the torso, the bridge between the hands
and eyes blown up senselessly
without thought. I know nothing
of the body's rebellion, the nights spent
lying in the streets, the small favors,
the long crowds of adulterers knocking
quietly on their own doors. We see only this
shadow of desire, an aimless hand,
an amputated arm, a wound that will not heal.

   •   •   •   •   •   •

One summer a man took off his clothes
in a crowded room. A thousand words
sprung from beneath his shirt, a long
tirade of air blew around his body
without mercy. The longest night
dug into his flesh like fingernails.
Later this man would invent the word 'decorum.'

   •   •   •   •   •   •

There is a season made of wax,
a hundred leaves falling into the hand,
the sun going down like a woman
on the oldest man. I would not give up
this moment for all the intelligence
reports on the body, the exact time
of its departure, its waking

from the grave, the slow rising
of the forehead like a message from the dead.

   •   •   •   •   •   •

When we open the letter of the body
it will be like the chair in which
we are sitting, the drink of water
sliding down the throat, the end
of the line between the bedroom
and the bedsheets. We will walk
on the edge of the longest balcony,
waving good-bye to the wilted flowers
of the spirit, the forgotten promise
of the language, the last words
always left unsaid.

The Great Chain of Being

All over this world there are hands
lying awake in the pockets under the dresses
hands are billowing out like sails
against the great masts of the thighs

there are so many hands full of cruelty
with lines in the palms deep as scars
the hands of the working man with the smell of salt
and the wealthy man who hides his hands
in the deepest folds of his wallet

there are the aimless hands of virgins
which are clouds drifting away from the body
the hands of promiscuity are everywhere
these hands are the lichens of the body
attaching themselves to everything
when I touch you my hands are like straw
any moment I expect them to go up in flame

the hands lead the body everywhere
hands are growing out of the ground
like hungry flowers they are growing
out of the flesh like ivy like iron
chains the hands surround us always shaking
waving good-bye reaching out for their brothers
cutting themselves off from loneliness

The Last Train of Thought

The trains go out again
but this time they are empty

this time there is a man in the last car
his arms are full of baggage
he wants to wave at the people
on the platform but the platform
is empty it worries him

all that waving
for nothing all that baggage
with his books and papers
in order what do they prove
now he doesn't even know

why the train keeps moving
off the tracks why it is leaving the ground

his letters scatter like old leaflets
his shoes are talking

when they hit the ground they are whispering
I am not going with him he wants
to rewrite everything
with a happy ending his friends
might understand wherever his friends might be

he wants to know why wouldn't they meet him
at the station it will be a long journey
without them

he has never traveled this way
without an explanation but the wheels
roll over his questions one by one
what friends what journey what ending

In the Butcher Shop

It is raining in the butcher shop
the sawdust floats to the top of the counters
the meat begins to turn
like the bodies from an ancient drowning
the butcher's knife is weeping with blood
in the water the blood is lost
the butcher is lost the wooden floor
forgets all its footprints everything
that is not water is not remembered

a customer swims by
he is unhappy with his last purchase
he tells the butcher each time he speaks
the water fills his body like a fountain
he begins to drown but he cannot stop himself
from speaking it is the curse of meat
to be buried in the word the butcher
nods in agreement each time he nods
his knife slices the water aimlessly
endlessly the water returns the knife
turns to rust the butcher turns to meat

it is raining in the butcher shop
and the whole world is weeping

The Return to Mysticism

When the rain returns

with its rope of water
the swirls of dust
will unwind

in our houses we are safe
from nothing but
what could surprise us

the broom that blossoms
in the pantry
the coats in the closets

growing their torsos
the cemeteries spilling over
into the bedrooms the dead

breaking the chains
the cold wires of their arms
beginning to bend again

we hear this music
wherever we turn it is this
old song what could be

more reasonable the gods
out of tune our prayers
unanswered as usual

we know what will happen
next the world turning
over in its grave the stars

going out one by one

Seance

She has been missing for years
but we find traces of her
everywhere in the tracks
of tires the curved wires
of the palms in the mirrors
of the mirrors. The table
rises in our hands like dough,
she speaks to us through the pores
of wood. *Open,* she says, *Open,*
and our tongues fly out
of our mouths like criminals,
our hearts squeeze out of the jail
of our ribs. When the body empties
itself like a bottle of wine, she
enters as air in a balloon, an unborn
child in the womb. And as we rise
out of this room like a spine
of smoke, we leave a char of bones
behind the mirror and a cloud
of flesh on the ceiling
for those who must remain.

On Meeting Robert Desnos in My Sleep

*Robert Desnos (1900–1945), French surrealist poet, who
died in a Nazi concentation camp.*

We meet in a concentration camp. It is late nineteen forty-
four, and the War is almost over. He takes me by the hand
and reads the future in my palm. He says I will never live
to see forty-eight, that I have no will left in my thumb, that
my fame-line is very faint. He does not believe my wife has
been faithful to me, but says that it does not really matter.
When he speaks, his voice is so low it is almost inaudible;
it is almost as though there were someone else speaking to
me, someone who was locked inside his body. When he
speaks to me, the concentration camp, our fellow prisoners,
even the sky which surrounds us, all seem to disappear. The
pupils of his eyes are like bowls which can contain me. They
frighten me more than all the Germans I have seen, so I close
my eyes and manage to awaken myself. For a brief moment
I am awake, looking straight up at the ceiling, which at first
glance looks like a wall on its side. But Desnos will not let me
go — he grabs me back into sleep by the throat. I feel the
sensation of suffocation. "It is not easy to leave me," he says,
"although we always try to return to the world that we know.
But me, I am more at home in this world than you are when
you walk into your local grocery. Only sometimes will you let
your mind wander there, say when you pick up a piece of
fruit and you let it become, or rather it itself becomes the skull
of a small animal. But I am this way all the time — for me, the
tomato is always inside the skull of a fox."

What is so strange about Desnos is that he says he is not
afraid of going crazy, of dying, or even of the Nazis who are
always watching him. "The Nazis are so easy to understand,"

70

he says. "They have no inner life. When you look into their eyes, or into the barrels of their Lugers, it is always at bottom the same thing. Sometimes the German believes his gun is only an extension of his hand, the barrel his longest, most hollow finger which he may point at anyone to escape from himself."

Desnos holds seances in his cell. He makes the table rise, the bed, even the hands of the cellmates who will not speak to him because they believe he is crazy. Desnos believes he can communicate with the dead, although he does not need to hear from them. What seems to frighten most of us, though, is his ability to disappear, or make us disappear from his consciousness. One moment someone may be speaking with him and the next moment he is in a trance. No one knows what he is thinking, where he is going: we only know we cannot reach him. It is this realization that makes him disappear. I am frightened, and I am no longer able to wake myself. And I am no longer in his cell with him, but in the middle of the night I am in an open field just outside the camp. A light shines on me and suddenly I am surrounded by Nazis again. In broken French a guard asks me what am I doing here. I tell him, "I do not know. I only know I do not belong here." "Ce n'est pas assez bon," he says. It is not good enough. He raises his hand to strike me with the butt of his gun, and the moment before he strikes me I can see inside the barrel. It is not quite a tunnel or an abyss, but it is almost as though I could see him hiding along the edges of that barrel. And when the gun goes off accidentally, I see arms floating in front of my face, a pair of eyes moving off toward the stars, and a large hand reaching for the back of my neck. I know I will never sleep again.